Steve Baker & Dieter Kropp

Blues Harping

Volume 1

00.091.125

MATTH. HOHNER AG

Trossingen · Deutschland

Contents

Foreword   3

CD Tracklisting   4

1. What is a Blues Harp?   5
   The different Models   6

2. How to hold the Harp   10
   How to play Single Notes   11
   Breathing and Intonation   12

3. Notes and Chords available on a C Harp   14
   The 12 bar blues form in C   16
   "Straight Harp" / 1st Position   17

4. "Cross Harp" / 2nd Position   18

5. Blue Notes, Bending   22

6. Important Playing Techniques   29

7. Positions 3 - 5   35

8. Amplification & Microphones   39

9. Influential Players   40

10. A Short Harp Discography   41

11. Playing with Other Musicians   50

12. Care and Maintenance   50

13. Further Reading   51

© 1989 & 1998 by Matth. Hohner AG Trossingen · Germany
All rights reserved
Revised and expanded 3rd edition 1998
Steve Baker & Dieter Kropp
Blues Harping, Volume 1
ISBN 3-920468-80-5 (German Version)
Cat.-No. 00.091.127 (German Version)
ISBN 3-920468-26-0 (English Version)
Cat.-No. 00.091.125 (English Version)

All photos that appear in this book are courtesy of "Harmonica Museum Trossingen/Germany"
and "Sparerips Records, Detmold/Germany".

This book summarizes the most important aspects of blues harp playing in an easily understandable form. It explains how the harmonica functions, and introduces the reader to important playing techniques through practical musical examples.

Although some of this information may be of use to the more advanced player, our main intention was to help the beginner to understand the blues harp, to make this mysterious and fascinating instrument more accessible, and to provide the necessary basis for further progress. We hope that we've succeeded in this, and wish all our readers a lot of fun playing.

Keep on Harping!

Steve Baker & Dieter Kropp 1997

Plakat of 1925

Track No. 32. - 60. German version

01.	Introduction Holding the Harp, Breathing	2'25"
02.	Playing single Notes	1'18"
03.	C major scale	0'23"
04.	Major pentatonic scale in C	0'21"
05.	The 12-bar-blues-form	1'01"
06.	"Straight Harp Blues" (Steve Baker) 12-bar-blues in C - Playback	1'22"
07.	"Cross Harp / 2nd Position"	1'39"
08.	"Cross Harp Blues" (Steve Baker) 12-bar-blues in G - Playback	1'40"
09.	"Don't Suck!" (Steve Baker) 12-bar-blues in G - Playback	1'44"
10.	"cross harp": Which harp for which key?	0'38"
11.	Bending	2'20"
12.	Blues Scale	0'47"
13.	Using the Blues Scale	0'20"
14.	"Blues Scale Blues" (Steve Baker) 12-bar-blues in G - Playback	1'56"
15.	"Bending Blues" (Steve Baker) 12-bar-blues in G - Playback	2'07"
16.	Hand Effects: Damping, Tremolo, Wah Wah	1'57"
17.	Vibrato	1'18"
18.	Trills	1'03"
19.	Double Notes	0'54"
20.	Octaving	0'57"
21.	Rhythmic Patterns	2'08"
22.	"Two Rhythm Licks" (Dieter Kropp)	0'31"
23.	"Chugging" (Steve Baker) rhythmic number in G - Playback	1'40"
24.	"3rd. Position"	1'45"
25.	"Make Mine A Minor" (Steve Baker) 12-bar-blues in D - Playback	1'49"
26.	4th Position scale/a-minor aeolian (natural minor)	0'20"
27.	5th Position scale/e-minor phrygian	0'23"

28.	Amplified blues harmonica: excerpt from "You Told Me" (Dieter Kropp/ Sordino Musikverlag), played on a Bb-Harp in the key of F, previously released on CD: "The Fabulous Barbecue Boys feat. Dieter Kropp -... doin' the blues", Spareribs Records SPR01, used equipment: '59 Fender Tube Bassman, '63 Fender Reverb, Hohner Blues Blaster	1'48"
29.	Afterword	0'22"
30.	"Blue Harp Swing" (Steve Baker/Hohner Musikverlag) -excerpt from new version- played on a C-Harp in the key of G previously released on CD: "Slow Roll" - Steve Baker & Chris Jones Acoustic Music Records 319.1070.2	2'00"
31.	"Two Harp Thing' (Steve Baker/Dieter Kropp) (GEMA / Manuskriptwerk) previously unreleased Wintermoor-Jam! played on two A-Harmonicas in the key of E	3'53"

You only need one harp in the key of "C" to play all of the tunes and exercises on this CD with the exception of "Two Harp Thing" (track 31) and "You Told Me" (track 28).

With all of the songs of this CD the harp is in the left hand channel and the guitar is in the right hand channel of your stereo, so that you can practice just with the guitar if you turn the stereo control full right.

One final point: some of the songs on the German language part differ slightly from the ones on the English part of this CD. You can play the same tunes to these backings, but the groove is different, so even if you don't understand the words you can play along to some different music. Check it out!

Total playing time: 79'40"

CD-premastering by Andreas Torkler and Dieter Kropp at Sonopress, Gütersloh/Germany

What exactly is meant by the expression "Blues Harp"? Well, the name originated in the USA, and is used as a collective term for all 10-hole single note diatonic harmonicas that are tuned according to the so-called "Richter" system. Joseph Richter was an early and extremely influential harmonica manufacturer from Haida in Bohemia, and around 1857 he developed a harmonica tuning system using only notes belonging to one major scale. The musical expression for this is "diatonic". This means that on a C harmonica you only find notes belonging to the C-major scale, on a G harmonica only notes belonging to the G-major scale, and so on. Because of this, you use different harps to play in different keys. The key of each instrument is stamped on the top cover plate or printed on the end of the comb. The diagram on page 14 shows how the notes are arranged.

Often this kind of harmonica is simply referred to as a "harp". One Hohner model is indeed called the "Blues Harp", but the name is generally used for any model constructed and tuned according to the Richter system. These are listed below with a brief description of each. The construction of this kind of harmonica is very simple:

The component parts of a diatonic harp

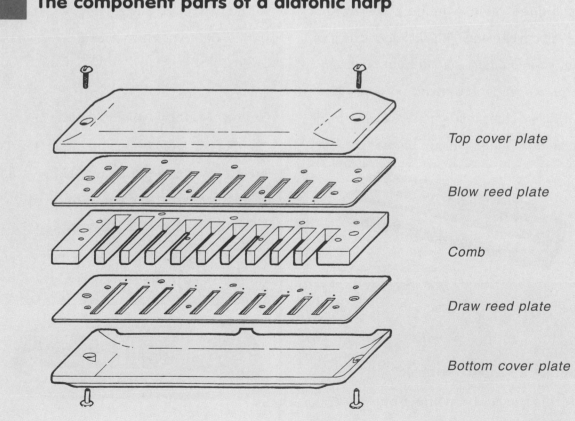

Top cover plate

Blow reed plate

Comb

Draw reed plate

Bottom cover plate

The harp's current widespread popularity basically began with the blues boom of the sixties, which opened the ears of white audiences to black American music for the first time on any large scale. Ever since, creative musicians have been finding ways to use the wonderful possibilities of this instrument to great effect in many other contexts. Today the blues harp can be heard in the most varied musical settings, from pop music to hard rock, from new wave to new age, from film soundtracks to country & western, from punk to funk and from folk to techno. Through its unmistakable (and often imitated!) sound and unique musical character, this inconspicuous little instrument has won a firm place in the hearts of millions of music fans the world over.

The Different Models

– Handmade

These instruments are crafted entirely by hand using painstaking traditional methods. The "classics"!

Marine Band M1896 "classic"

This harp has been the standard blues harmonica ever since 1896, and is still going strong over 100 years later! One of the biggest selling models worldwide. Curved cover plates with side openings give it its characteristic sound, both bright and warm, which can be heard on virtually all the classic blues recordings. Available in all major keys, natural minor, harmonic minor,

Marine Band M1896 "classic"

plus high G, Low F#, low F, low E, low Eb & low D.

Special 20 M560 "classic"

The plastic body of the Special 20 is extremely airtight, and cannot swell up when moistened by playing, which is easy on the lips. Cover plates with closed sides ensure a warm, even tone. The plastic bodied equivalent (also in popularity) of the Marine Band 1896. Available in all major keys.

Golden Melody M542 "classic"

The Golden Melody boasts ergonomically formed cover plates with closed sides and a wine red plastic comb. The tempered tuning (i.e. each octave is divided into twelve equal steps) ensures that it is always in tune with other instruments, whatever key they

Golden Melody M542 "classic"

may be playing in. Ideal for single note playing, and the harmonica of choice of overblow master Howard Levy, the Golden Melody is the only Hohner diatonic model to be tuned in this way. Available in all major keys.

Marine Band M364 and M365

Both these big Marine Bands are tuned one octave lower than usual in C, and are popular among harp players for rhythmic numbers thanks to their full chord sound. Sonny Boy Williamson II used them for some of his finest recordings. Available in C and G.

Marine Band M365

Marine Band M365 SBS "Extended bending range"

By extending the tonal range of the instrument downwards without altering the configuration of the notes, the "Steve Baker Special" permits the typical bluesy bends over a range of 2 1/2 instead of 1 1/2 octaves. This makes it possible to play many standard riffs over a much wider range than is possible on any other harmonica model. Available in C, D, F, G & A.

Marine Band Soloist M364/60

"Solo tuning" - this harp is tuned just like a chromatic harmonica, but has no slide. It is excellent for playing in 3rd position, a popular style for blues chromatic, and many of the notes can be bent exactly as on a diatonic harp. Available in C major only.

- Modular System "MS"

The abbreviation "MS" stands for Modular System, a completely new concept in harmonica design from Hohner. It comprises innovations which not only improve the playing characteristics, but also make handling and maintenance a great deal easier. All parts (comb, reed plates, cover plates) are fully compatible amongst all different models, and are available separately as spares, enabling the player to adapt the instrument to suit his or her individual preferences. All parts are fixed together with screws, allowing easy assembly and disassembly, and are produced on Hohner's fully automated computer controlled production line, the first of its kind in the world, which works with an unparalleled degree of precision and consistency.

Blues Harp MS M533

The Blues Harp MS has a wooden comb and standard reed plates 0.9mm in thickness. The extra-stable cover plates are curved with closed sides, giving a warm sound. Available in all major keys.

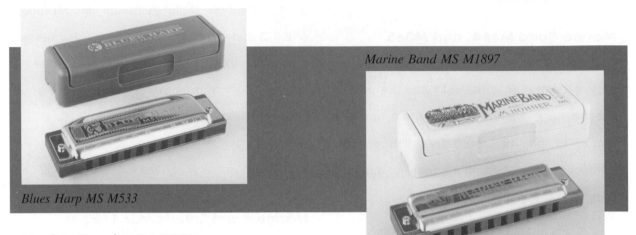

Marine Band MS M1897

Blues Harp MS M533

Marine Band MS M1897

The Marine Band MS also has a wooden comb and 0.9mm reed plates, but the cover plates are open at the sides, giving the sound more overtones and making the overall tone brighter and more powerful. All major keys.

Big River Harp MS M590

A great low-price instrument using MS components to create an ideal introduction to the MS series. Open-sided Marine Band cover plates and black plastic comb give a powerful, even tone. All major keys plus high G, low F#, low F, low E, low Eb and low D.

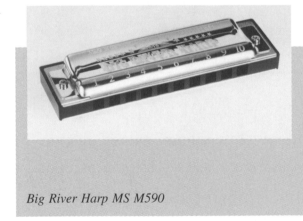

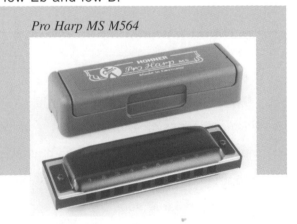

Pro Harp MS M564

Big River Harp MS M590

Pro Harp MS M564

Black anodized cover plates with closed sides, similar to the Blues Harp MS, 0.9mm reed plates and a black plastic comb give the Pro Harp MS a rounder, more neutral sound. Available in a variety of special tunings (Natural Minor, Harmonic Minor, Country Tuning, high G, low F#, low F, low E, low E^b and low D) as well as in all major keys.

Cross Harp MS M566

Gold plated plastic comb and black anodized cover plates with closed sides are combined with extra-thick reed plates (1.05mm) for more punch and a brighter sound. Available in C, D, E, F, G, A, Bb, B.

Meisterklasse MS M581

Cross Harp MS M566

Meisterklasse MS M581

Hohner's luxury model! Extra-thick 1.05mm nickel plated reed plates to minimise air loss are mounted on an aluminium comb and enclosed in chrome plated cover plates with a unique form-fitting design ensuring a clear, powerful tone. All major keys.

Special Model:

Slide Harp M7312/Chromatic Koch M980

These two models offer a unique combination of the diatonic Richter harmonica with the chromatic. As with all chromatics, a slide permits each note to be raised by one semitone; however, as the instrument is either not valved (Koch) or only partially valved (Slide Harp) against air loss, it is possible to bend notes exactly as on the diatonic. These harps are tuned according to the Richter system and offer the harp player chromatic scales combined with bluesy sounds. Available in C and G only.

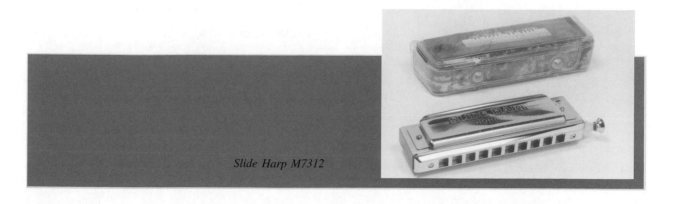

Slide Harp M7312

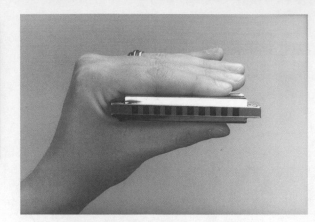

Photo 1 - The simplest and most effective way to hold the harp is between index finger and thumb of the left hand.

The simplest and most effective way is to take the harp between index finger and thumb of the left hand, with the low notes to the left, resting that end of the instrument against the point where thumb and index finger join (see photo 1). In this way, the right hand can be used to modify the sound and create a variety of effects. It's important not to hold the harp too near the front, as you then won't have enough space to put your lips around the mouthpiece! The fingers should grip the harp towards the back so that it projects forward slightly (see photo 2), and it helps if the index finger is curved so that it doesn't lie flat across the back of the harp where it might get in the way of your lips.

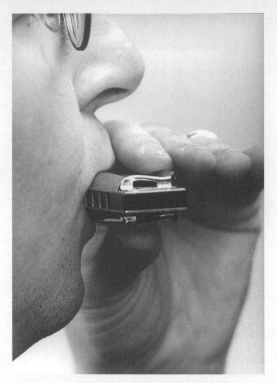

Photo 2 - If the fingers grip the harp towards the back of the cover plates, the lips can enclose the mouthpiece more comfortably.

If you've already got used to holding the harp in your right hand (with the low notes to the right!), there's no real need to change now. Well known players such as harmonica legends Sonny Terry and Paul Butterfield also do this; the main thing is that you feel comfortable when playing, and that your grip is relaxed but firm.

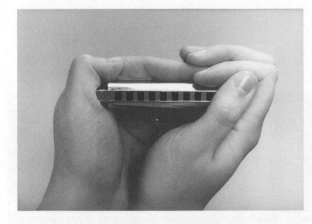

Photo 3 - Many blues players also hold the harp as pictured left. The most important thing is that you feel comfortable and relaxed when playing.

Playing Single Notes

The harmonica works according to the principle of the free reed. The reeds are fixed at one end only so that they can vibrate in the airstream caused by blowing (exhaling) or drawing (inhaling) through the channel openings. This is what produces the sound.

It's important not to breathe too hard or use too much air, because then the notes may not sound clearly or at the right pitch. It's also very important to avoid any air loss between your lips and the harp, as this reduces volume and interrupts the airflow, which has a negative effect on the sound. Air loss can often be heard as a slight hiss.

The first step towards mastering the harp is to learn to play single notes. Almost all other techniques build on this one, so there's no way around learning it! There are two basic ways of doing this, of which the simpler is usually known as

-Lip Blocking

Form your lips as if to whistle a low note, and place them over the mouthpiece of the harp so that they only enclose one hole. It's helpful to try whistling while drawing (inhaling) to get the right embouchure.

The mouth position is slightly open - don't clench your teeth - and the harp should be enclosed by the moist inner part of your lips, not the dry outer part. The instrument is meant to be in the mouth, not in front of it! This is vital for an uninterrupted airflow and loud, clear notes, which require a resonance space inside the mouth in order to sound. Now breathe gently through the harp, both blowing and drawing. If you hear more than one note at the same time, try moving the harp slightly

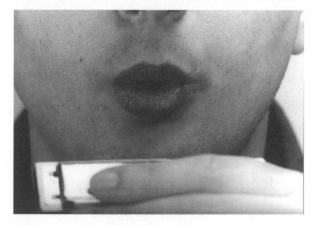

When lip blocking you have to form your lips as if to whistle a low note. Try to relax!

to one side without breaking the contact with the lips until you only hear a single tone. You need to actually grasp the harp with your lips, so that the corners of your mouth can complete the seal around the channel you're playing, thus preventing any air escaping. Try to relax your facial muscles while doing all this - if they become tense then take a break and let them loosen up!

The other method of playing single notes is known as

-Tongue Blocking,

and is used a great deal in traditional harmonica styles. Here the mouth opening is wider, so that the lips can enclose several channels at once - three or four is the usual number. In order to play a single note, the tongue is used to cover (block) the lower holes, so that the airstream can only pass through the one on the right, thus sounding the highest of the enclosed notes. For example, the lips enclose holes 2, 3 and 4. The tongue is used to cover 2 and 3 so that the 4th channel can sound on its own.

Though this technique is more difficult to master, many blues harpists prefer it because you get a fuller, warmer tone in this way. Little Walter, Big Walter Horton and Rod Piazza are masters of this style.

The first method is more suitable for the beginner, but long term it's worthwhile trying to learn both, as you can then use them to vary your tone, and your playing will become more expressive and varied. Lipping generally sounds harder, whereas tongue blocking sounds smoother; by combining these techniques you have a wider spectrum of tonal possibilities open to you, and can use them to influence the character of a melody or a solo.

Breathing and Intonation

Correct intonation - getting the notes to sound at the right pitch - is very important for a good sound; one of the biggest difficulties encountered by beginners is to prevent the lower draw notes from sounding flat (too low). This is almost always due to the fact that the space inside the mouth is too small. The shape of the inside of the mouth plays a big role here: the lips should enclose the front of the harp so that the jaws can remain slightly open, and only the moist inner part of the lips is in contact with the instrument. Try and keep the space inside your mouth as large as possible - if you purse your lips and try to suck the notes out, they will definitely sound flat!

CD-Track 01

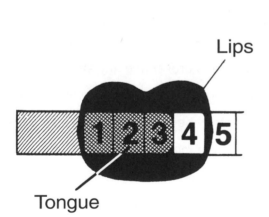

Lips

Tongue

Try to always breathe in a relaxed manner from the diaphragm, and don't use more air than necessary. You need to learn to breathe slowly and deeply in and out, so that you can feel your diaphragm tensing and relaxing, and the belly moves in and out. This is very similar to breathing techniques used in yoga or meditation, and makes the airflow much easier to control. **Whatever you do, don't suck!!** If you can learn to play the harmonica at the same time you've killed two birds with one stone!

Junior Wells

Whichever model you choose, it's advisable to start on a harp in the key of C, which lies in the middle of the available pitch range; for this reason it's usually the easiest key for the beginner. All the musical examples in this book and the accompanying CD were played on a harp in C. The notes are arranged as follows:

The Basic Notes and Chords of the Diatonic Richter Harp in C:

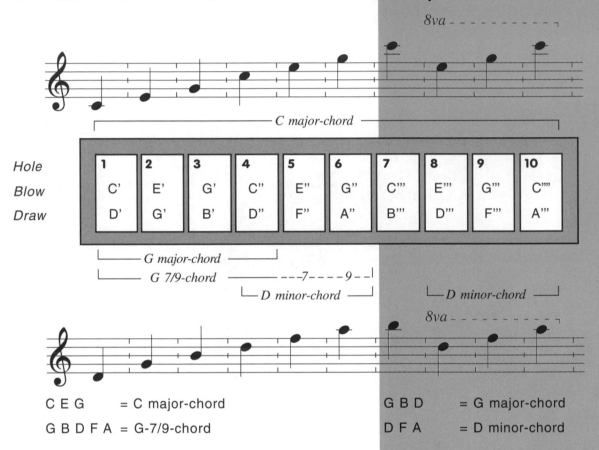

| CEG | = C major-chord | | GBD | = G major-chord |
| GBDFA | = G-7/9-chord | | DFA | = D minor-chord |

All of the notes shown below belong to the C major scale. In the case of harps in other keys, the notes are always ordered according to the same principle. The pitch will be higher or lower, depending on the key, but the relationship of the notes in each hole to one another remains the same. This type of arrangement is called "diatonic", and only contains notes belonging to the major scale to which the instrument is tuned. The range is three octaves. The central octave (holes 4-7) contains a complete major scale. Here it is usually written one octave lower than it sounds (indicated by the symbol 8va). This makes it easier to read music for the harmonica.

For all of the written exercises in this book we use the following tablature in addition to the notation:

↑ = B l o w   ↓ = D r a w (hole number as given)

CD-Track 03

CD-Track 04

CD-Track 05

The C major Scale

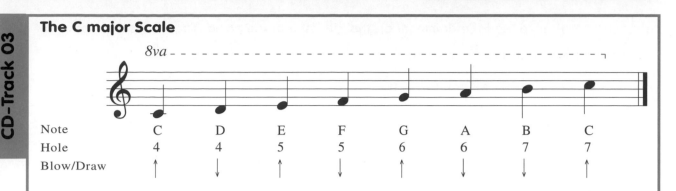

Note	C	D	E	F	G	A	B	C
Hole	4	4	5	5	6	6	7	7
Blow/Draw	↑	↓	↑	↓	↑	↓	↓	↑

Try playing the sequence of notes shown above one after the other. They make up a C major scale, which is only present in its entirety in the central octave, and provides an ideal starting point for the beginning player.

In the bottom octave (holes 1-4) F´ and A´ are missing (the 4th and 6th notes of the scale); in the top octave (holes 7-10) the 7th, B´´´, is missing. However, it's possible to play G´ in the bottom octave by drawing (hole 2) <u>or</u> by blowing (hole 3). The reason for this anomaly lies in the harmonic structure of the instrument - G is a vital part of both the blow chord C major <u>and</u> the draw chord G7. Here is an exercise to help you get used to how the notes are arranged in the middle octave, and to practice playing single notes. Don't try to play it too quickly, it's better to concentrate on making the individual notes sound clearly. Remember to breathe deeply and slowly!

Pentatonic scale in C major

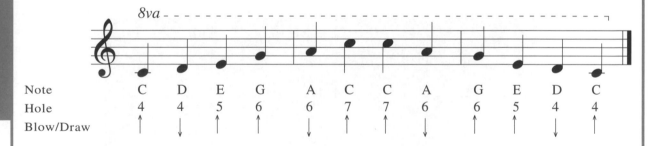

Note	C	D	E	G	A	C	C	A	G	E	D	C
Hole	4	4	5	6	6	7	7	6	6	5	4	4
Blow/Draw	↑	↓	↑	↑	↓	↑	↑	↓	↑	↑	↓	↑

This pentatonic scale consists of five notes from the C major scale - the fourth and seventh notes are missing. It's a great basis for improvisation, and is the oldest known type of scale.

When practicing these scales, you may find that you stumble upon fragments of well known melodies - folk songs, children's songs or shanties are mostly played in the central octave.

It's very useful to know how the available chords on the harp relate to one another. The harmonic structure of most blues music is based on the three main chords derived from the notes of the major scale: they are known as the tonic, subdominant and dominant chords. The tonic starts on the first note or step of the scale, and is the root chord in that key. We find the subdominant on the fourth step, and the dominant on the fifth step of the scale. They are constructed as follows (example in C):

Chords derived from a C major scale

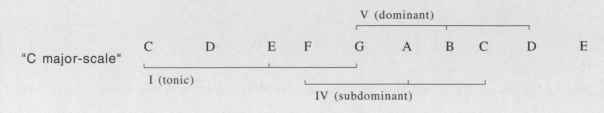

C major = C E G (tonic or I chord)

F major = F A C (subdominant or IV chord)

G major = G B D (dominant or V chord)

Many other styles of music apart from blues are based on these three chords - most English and American folk songs, for example, and many rock and pop numbers. Many blues tunes share a common harmonic structure or chord sequence called the 12 bar blues form, which you will almost certainly recognize when you hear it even if you didn't know what it was called before. This is repeated throughout the song from beginning to end. Here is the chord sequence (numbered from bar 1 to bar 12) for a typical 12 bar blues in C.

1 C_I	2 C_I	3 C_I	4 C^7_I
5 F_{IV}	6 F_{IV}	7 C_I	8 C_I
9 G^7_V	10 F_{IV}	11 C_I	12 G^7_V

I = tonic, IV = subdominant, V = dominant 7th

This type of chord sequence or structure is frequently the basis for an entire song - most blues numbers consist of a verse structure like this which is simply repeated as often as necessary, and serves as the accompaniment for vocals and solos.

In order to be able to play along with a blues, you need to get accustomed to the way that the 12 bar form sounds, and where the chord changes come, so that you can anticipate what's going to happen next. The best way to do this is to listen to as much of this type of music as possible! Try to follow the chord changes played by the accompanying instruments. Learn to recognize where one verse ends, and the next one begins. With practice you'll find that you get a feeling for this structure, so that you know where you are in it at any given point, and can begin to play along with it. You're doing what generations of harp players have done before you - learning through listening, feeling and experimenting. Remember though, listening comes first!

Here is a 12 bar blues in C to practice on. The harp is played in the key to which it's tuned, and the melody is all in the central octave. Try to get to know the length of the individual lines, and the length of the verse. Listen to the version on the CD, practice the melody and let the rhythm guitar carry you through the song!

"Straight Harp Blues" / Steve Baker

- 12 bar blues in C - 1st position -

Chords	C			C	C⁷
Note	G	F E F E C	C		
Hole	6	5 5 5 5 4	4		
Blow/Draw	↑	↓ ↑ ↓ ↑ ↑	↑		

Chords	F	F	C	C
Note	C	A G A	G	
Hole	7	6 6 6		
Blow/Draw	↑	↓ ↑ ↓	↑	

Chords	G⁷	F	C	G⁷
Note	G	F E F E	C	
Hole	6	5 5 5 5	4	
Blow/Draw	↑	↓ ↑ ↓ ↑	↑	

Playing on a C harp in C is called "straight harp" or 1st position.

Even though this tune could almost be a typical Louisiana swamp blues, you're still no doubt wondering if this is the real deal. Yes, there has to be more to it than that! Although the harp was originally designed to be played mainly in the central octave, and in the key of the major

3 | "straight harp" or 1st Position ● ● ● ● ● ● ● ● ● ● ●

scale to which it's tuned, the beauty of the Richter system is that it offers other possibilities as well. The history of the instrument has taken a number of strange turnings which would definitely have surprised its inventor. The first Richter harmonicas arrived in the USA in the late 19th century, where black musicians were almost certainly the first to discover the magical quality that the lower draw notes possessed. They found that the pitch of these notes could be lowered by up to three semitones, and that the possibilities of modulating the tone were far greater than on the blow notes. They discovered a whole new world of musical expression in the instrument which had hitherto been unknown, and which was far more appropriate to their musical culture and lifestyle. Through trial and error a new way of playing the harp emerged: the blues style, often known as "cross harp" or 2nd position.

4 | "cross harp" or 2nd Position ● ● ● ● ● ● ● ● ● ● ●

CD-Track 07

If you look at how the notes of the C major scale are arranged on the harp, you'll see that only two of the three main chords in C (as discussed in the previous chapter) can be played in their entirety: tonic (I, C major) and dominant (V, G 7th). This means that chord accompaniment over all three chords is not possible. If however you take advantage of the tonal layout of the diatonic Richter harp, and try playing in the key of the draw chord (G7th) instead of in the key of the blow chord (C major), the whole thing looks very different. This is what is meant by the expression "cross harp" or "2nd position" - you play the same notes, belonging to the C major scale, but you take a G note as your starting point instead of a C. The resulting sequence is known as a G-mixolydian or dominant 7th scale:

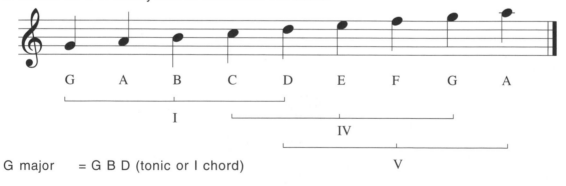

G major   = G B D (tonic or I chord)

C major   = C E G (subdominant or IV chord)

D minor   = D F A (dominant or V chord)

Now all three main chords can be played as such on the harp: tonic G, subdominant C and dominant D. The D chord is minor (F is the minor third in D), but blues gets a lot of its typical sound from playing minor thirds over major chords, so this is no problem. Two of the above chords are draw chords - G and D - and the vital thing you need to remember about cross harp is that here the most important notes are to be found in the lower draw channels. Your root note G is the draw note in hole 2, and all of the first five draw notes are closely related to the G7 chord (which they produce when played together), the root chord of the cross harp key. The easiest way to express this is to say that in 1st position you play in the key of the blow chord, whereas in 2nd position you play in the key of the draw chord.

Here is a typical chord sequence for a 12 bar blues in G:

1	2	3	4
G_I	G_I	G_I	G^7_I
5	**6**	**7**	**8**
C_{IV}	C_{IV}	G_I	G_I
9	**10**	**11**	**12**
D^7_V	C_{IV}	G_I	D^7_V

I = tonic, IV = subdominant, V = dominant 7th

To get used to playing "crossed", try playing the melody of "Straight Harp Blues" on page 17 in 2nd position on a C harp. The tune is transposed from C to G - i.e. the melody sounds the same, and you use the same harp, only the key in which you play is different.

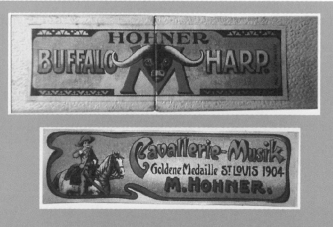

"Pioneer" - 1930s label from the Hotz company, who were also pioneers in spreading the message of the harmonica. Hohner bought them out in 1906, but continued manufacturing and marketing Hotz harmonicas until 1980.

"Cross Harp Blues" / Steve Baker

- 12 Bar Blues in G - 2nd Position -

Chords	G	G			G	G⁷

First line:

Chords	G				G	G⁷
Note	D		C B C B	G/G\	G/G\	
Hole	4		4 3 4 3	2(3	2(3	
Blow/Draw	↓		↑ ↓ ↑ ↓	↓(↑↑	↓(↑	

Chords	C	C		G	G
Note	G		E D E	D	
Hole	6		5 4 5	4	
Blow/Draw	↑		↑ ↓ ↑	↓	

Chords	D⁷	C		G	D⁷
Note	D		C B C B	G (G	
Hole	4		4 3 4 3	2 (3	
Blow/Draw	↓		↑ ↓ ↑ ↓	↓ (↑	

As you see, it's possible to play the same tune in different keys on the same harp.

In the tablature we have indicated that you can use 3 blow as an alternative to 2 draw for the bottom G note. Advanced players will mostly use 2 draw. Many beginners have difficulty playing this note with the correct intonation, though - it often sounds flat (too low), and doesn't have a pleasant sound. Please note that this is not usually the fault of the instrument, but of a wrong playing technique. What happens is that if the space inside your mouth is too small, then the wavelength of the note being played doesn't have enough room to resonate there, and the airflow also inhibits the reed. You need to keep your vocal tract (the space inside your mouth and throat) <u>as open as possible</u> while playing to counteract this. **This point is very important and cannot be over-emphasized!** It can be a great help to try whistling the note (especially while inhaling) before trying to play it. Think of how wide your throat opens when you yawn! If you practice playing 2 draw using these tips as a guide, you'll soon learn to get the correct intonation, and it will help your overall sound too!

When experimenting with melodies, riffs or improvisation in the cross harp style, it is a very good idea to try to end on one of the bottom draw notes, because you are then clearly using the draw chord as your tonal center. You're then no longer playing in C on your C harp, but in G. This is another reason to orient yourself around 2 draw as your root and ending note.

The majority of blues playing in 2nd position / cross harp uses the area between 2 draw and 6 blow (g´- g´´).

Here's another exercise which has a typical bluesy character:

"Don't Suck!" / Steve Baker

- 12 Bar Blues in G - 2nd Position -

) From this point onwards we have deliberately left out the sub-headings "chord, note, channel, blow/draw". The order of the symbols in the musical examples remains constant.

In order to find the right harp for a particular song when playing "crossed" / 2nd position, you can use the following system: If you know the key of the song (e.g. G), then go <u>four</u> notes up the scale (in this case G, A, B, <u>C</u>), and that's the key of harp you need. If you have a harp (e.g. in C) and want to know what key you're in when playing crossed, then go <u>five</u> notes up in the appropriate scale (C, D, E, F, <u>G</u>), and you have your key. This works for every harp and every key, as you can see from the table on page 38.

CD-Track 09

CD-Track 10

Perhaps the simplest method, however, uses the circle of 5ths. If you know the key of the harp, you proceed one step in a clockwise direction to find the cross harp key; if you know the key of the song, and want to know which harp you need, proceed one step in an anti-clockwise direction, and you have the key of the harp.

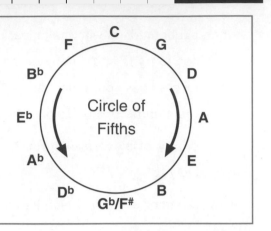

5 Blue Notes, Bending

CD-Track 11

One of the most important musical characteristics of the blues, and of all related forms of music such as rock, country or jazz, is the use of the so-called "blue notes". These notes lie in between the notes of the major scale and frequently have a very poignant "minor" character, although they can be played over major chords. The following figure shows the blue notes in relation to the scales in C and G which are available on a C harp:

1		2		3	4		5		6		7	8	C major scale
C	C#	D	E♭	E	F	F#	G	A♭	A	B♭	B	C	chromatic
			*			*				*			blue notes

1		2		3	4		5		6	7		8	G mixolydian
G	A♭	A	B♭	B	C	C#	D	E♭	E	F	F#	G	chromatic
			*			*				*			blue notes

If you play in the key of C on a C harp, i.e. in 1st position, then none of the blue notes are present. When playing in G (2nd position) however, one of them - F, 5 draw - is already available. This is what gives the previous song its bluesy character: the F in 5 draw plays a prominent role in the melody throughout the entire piece!

The other blue notes in G can be produced by a technique of immeasurable importance to blues harp playing known as "bending", which means lowering the pitch of certain notes so that they sound up to 3 semitones lower than normal. Bending is the single

"Big" Golden Wheeler

most important aspect of blues harmonica, and has to be mastered by anyone who wants to progress further on the instrument.

It is a unique feature of the Richter harmonica that every channel contains two reeds of different pitch, one of which normally only sounds when you blow, and the other of which normally only sounds when you draw. In both cases, some air is lost through the slot of the other reed, since the slots are not fitted with valves (windsavers) as in the case of the chromatic harmonica.

This is what makes bending possible, though, because it enables both reeds in a given channel to vibrate simultaneously in the same airstream. The way to lower the pitch of a bendable note (they can't all be bent!) is to alter the shape of the inside of your mouth and vocal tract. This effect is possible on the higher of the two notes in every channel, irrespective of whether that note is blow or draw (see chart on page 25, "Notes that can be produced by Bending"), and is easiest to achieve when the pitch difference between blow and draw reed is 2 semitones. The bottom six draw notes (the most important cross harp notes!) and the top four blow notes can all be bent down to a greater or lesser degree.

Most people find that bending draw notes is easier than bending blow notes, and it's also more useful, so we'll start there. Here's what to do:

It's best to begin on 4 draw. First of all you have to play the single note 4 draw, cleanly and without air loss, with plenty of space inside your mouth and throat. While breathing in, try altering the shape at the back of your tongue as if you were forming the silent vowels AAAAA-OOOOO-AAAAA-OOOOO. Don't break the contact between harp and lips when doing this. It's not necessary to draw any harder, but simply to find the right mouth and throat form. If you do this correctly, the note will sound lower when you change the form to OOOOO, and revert to its normal pitch on AAAAA. You'll notice that the airflow changes, and the further down you bend the note, the smaller the space at the front of your mouth becomes, and the larger the space at the back of the tongue. The whole effect really takes place in the throat, and not at the front of your mouth.

Another way of learning to bend is to try whistling the note and then lowering its pitch while inhaling. The tongue position here is really very similar to that used in bending, so this can also be well worth trying. In both cases it is vital that you start with a clean single note. If you have difficulties with this on 4 draw, you may find it easier to start learning this technique on 1 draw.

The Golden Rule

It is only possible to bend the <u>higher</u> of the two notes in any hole, irrespective of whether that note is a draw note (holes 1-6) or a blow note (holes 7-10). It can be bent down to a point just under a semitone above the lower note, and no further. The lower note in a given hole <u>cannot</u> be bent in this way.

This means that it's also possible to bend the upper blow notes, although this is more difficult than bending the lower draw notes. To bend a high blow note, form your lips as if you were whistling a high note, with the tongue behind the bottom row of teeth, and whilst blowing reduce the space at the front of your mouth (raise lower jaw slightly) and press down with your upper lip. However, the modulation of the notes is caused by changing the form of the vocal tract at the base of the tongue, as in draw bending, and not in the first instance by the lips and tip of the tongue. It's not necessary to blow harder to achieve this effect, but you have to maintain a higher air pressure than you need on draw bends, which is why you press down with the upper lip. Try this on holes 8 or 9 blow.

CAUTION! 5 draw and 7 blow can only be bent a small amount due to the fact that draw and blow notes in these channels are only one semitone apart. Trying to force them will damage your instrument and cause these notes to go out of tune!

The symbols for bent notes

The following exercises all make use of bent notes. In the tablature they are designated as follows:

Draw note, bent one semitone	↘
Draw note, bent one whole tone	↘
Draw note, bent three semitones	↘
Blow note, bent one semitone	↗
Blow note, bent one whole tone	↗

Notes that can be produced by bending

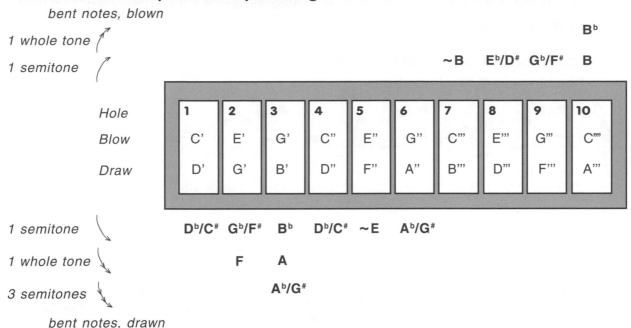

bent notes, blown

| | | | | | | | | | | B♭ |
| *1 whole tone* ↗ | | | | | | | | ~B | E♭/D♯ | G♭/F♯ | B |

| *1 semitone* ↗ | | | | | | | | | | |

Hole	**1**	**2**	**3**	**4**	**5**	**6**	**7**	**8**	**9**	**10**
Blow	C'	E'	G'	C''	E''	G''	C'''	E'''	G'''	C''''
Draw	D'	G'	B'	D''	F''	A''	B'''	D'''	F'''	A'''

1 semitone ↘	D♭/C♯	G♭/F♯	B♭	D♭/C♯	~E	A♭/G♯				
1 whole tone ↘		F	A							
3 semitones ↘			A♭/G♯							

bent notes, drawn

With plenty of practice you can learn to play the bent notes both as clean semitone intervals, and also as glissandi (slides). It's also possible (and extremely useful!) to hit the note when already bent down, and slide up to the normal pitch. The missing blue notes in G can be produced on a C harp by bending:

CD-Track 12

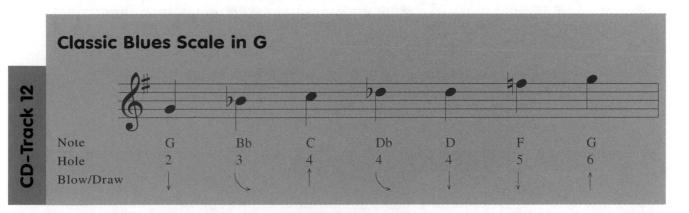

Classic Blues Scale in G

Note	G	Bb	C	Db	D	F	G
Hole	2	3	4	4	4	5	6
Blow/Draw	↓	↘	↑	↘	↓	↓	↑

CD-Track 13

The classic blues scale contains all three blue notes: the minor third Bb in channel 3 draw, the diminished fifth Db in 4 draw (both produced by bending one semitone) and the minor 7th F in 5 draw. The great thing about this scale is that it sounds good over all three chords used in the standard 12 bar blues. You can also find these blue notes in other places on the harp, for example the F produced by bending 2 draw. Take a look at the chart showing the bendable notes, and notice where they can be found on the instrument. This will help you learn which channels you need to work on in order to get your harp to sound bluesy!

Here is a 12 bar blues in G, in which the notes of the blues scale are played in sequence from top to bottom over all chords.

"Blues Scale Blues" / Steve Baker
- 12 bar blues in G, 2nd position -

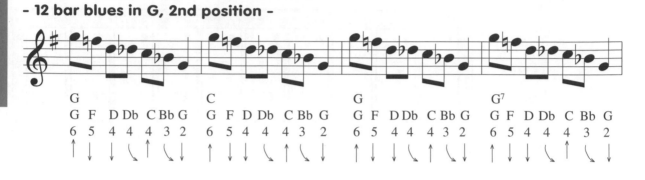

G	C	G	G⁷
G F D Db C Bb G	G F D Db C Bb G	G F D Db C Bb G	G F D Db C Bb G
6 5 4 4 4 3 2	6 5 4 4 4 3 2	6 5 4 4 4 3 2	6 5 4 4 4 3 2

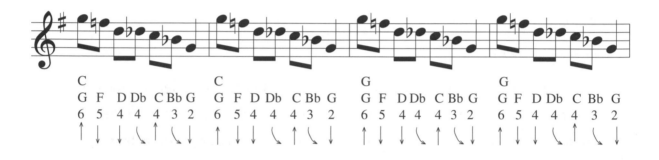

C	C	G	G
G F D Db C Bb G	G F D Db C Bb G	G F D Db C Bb G	G F D Db C Bb G
6 5 4 4 4 3 2	6 5 4 4 4 3 2	6 5 4 4 4 3 2	6 5 4 4 4 3 2

D⁷	C	G	G	D⁷
G F D Db C Bb G	G F D Db C Bb G	G F D Db C Bb G	G D D D	
6 5 4 4 4 3 2	6 5 4 4 4 3 2	6 5 4 4 4 3 2	2 1 1 1	

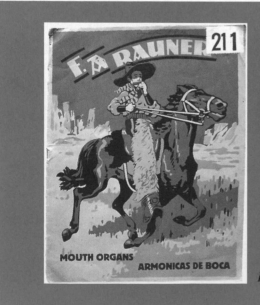

Rauner company catalogue cover, 1920s.

The two following scales are also extremely useful:

Mixolydian Scale in G

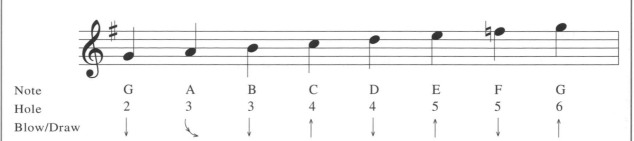

Note	G	A	B	C	D	E	F	G
Hole	2	3	3	4	4	5	5	6
Blow/Draw	↓	↘	↓	↑	↓	↑	↓	↑

This consists of the notes of the C major scale using G instead of C as the starting point, and is called the mixolydian or dominant 7th scale. The next scale is G major pentatonic. We have already encountered this scale in C on page 15.

Major Pentatonic Scale in G

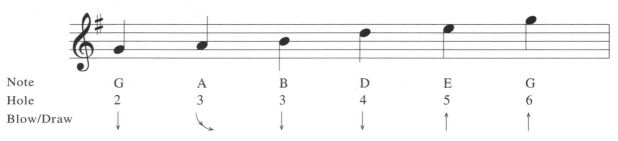

Note	G	A	B	D	E	G
Hole	2	3	3	4	5	6
Blow/Draw	↓	↘	↓	↓	↑	↑

In practice, these scales are often freely mixed together, and are used as a starting point for improvisations of all kinds. The vast majority of blues numbers are played in 2nd position (crossed), for example in G on a C harp or in E on an A harp, and make extensive use of bending and the scales shown above.

When playing along with another musician or a playback tape, first of all try to get used to the chord changes by playing the root note of each chord (see diagram "Basic Notes and Chords on the diatonic Richter Harmonica in C", page 14). When you know how the changes go, you can start using the scales shown above as a basis for improvisation, and try to fit them into the chord sequence. You'll find that lots of things will start to sound really good once you've practiced playing in 2nd position for a while. Not only the chords, but also many "blues licks" only start to sound good when you feel at home in this position.

The overwhelming majority of blues riffs are played in 2nd position or "crossed" on the harp, because many of the important notes in the cross harp mode are draw notes, which can be bent down to create a bluesy sound, and can be combined with the playing techniques described in the following chapter to good effect. Here is a song which uses bending to produce blue notes.

CD-Track 15

"Bending Blues" / Steve Baker

- 12 Bar Blues in G, 2nd Position, with Bending and Blue Notes -

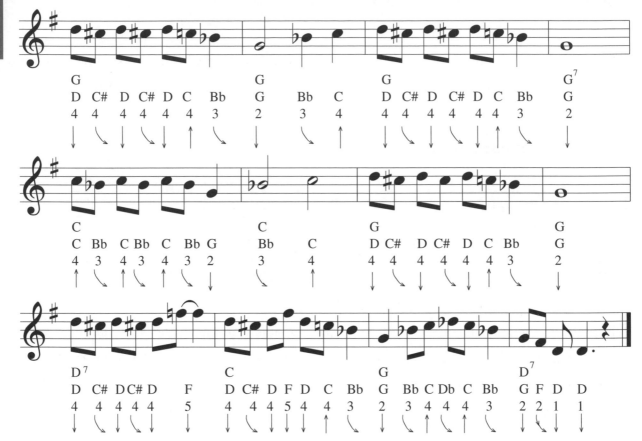

For a detailed description of the complex phenomenon of bending, as well as much additional information and practice exercises, see The "Harp Handbook" by Steve Baker (English edition), distributed by Music Sales/Hohner. For further practice material in the form of complete titles in notation and tablature with playback CD see "Blues Harping, Vol. 2" (English/German, Hohner Verlag).

HAND EFFECTS: DAMPING

The way in which the hands are cupped around the harp has a great influence on forming the individual player's tone - no two harmonica players sound exactly alike! The hands form a sort of resonance chamber around the harp, and the free hand is used to

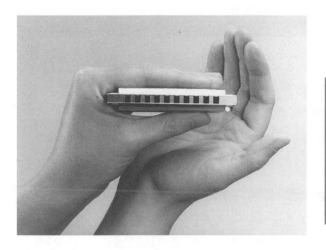

open or close this like a filter to a greater or lesser degree, depending on the type of sound required. Closing the hands creates a darker, more muffled tone, whereas opening them makes the sound brighter. There are various possibilities which lie in between, and one of the exciting things as you progress on the instrument is learning to use them in order to

create a more varied feeling to what you play by varying the character of the tone. It's not unlike the use of light and shade in painting. Try it!

A number of the following effects are created by using the hands.

VIBRATO

There are two main forms of vibrato: throat vibrato and diaphragm vibrato. It's important to master one of these techniques, as vibrato makes the sound of the instrument smoother and more pleasant to the ear. By rapidly lowering and raising the pitch of the note very slightly, it takes the edge off high notes, and makes the low ones sound fuller and warmer.

a) Throat Vibrato

The typical rough tough blues vibrato. You have to form a sort of silent "Ah" or "H" (as in harp) in the larynx while inhaling. This briefly interrupts the note. Keep drawing, and form a continuous sequence of "Ahs". The larynx produces a kind of controlled staccato, and the speed of the vibrato depends on how fast or slow this is. Throat vibrato works best on bendable draw notes.

b) Diaphragm Vibrato

Here the vibrato is produced by rapidly tensing and relaxing the diaphragm. The movement is not unlike that which occurs when panting, but of course the airflow is in one direction only. The speed of the vibrato is dictated by the speed of the diaphragm movement. Diaphragm vibrato works equally well on draw or on blow notes.

In both cases it's most important that the speed of the vibrato should be related to the rhythm of the music.

CD-Track 16

TREMOLO

The hands are cupped around the harp to form a more or less closed resonance chamber. By rapidly opening and closing this chamber with the hand which isn't holding the harp you can produce the tremolo effect, a fluttery, floating tone (which is occasionally wrongly referred to as vibrato). The hands are not generally closed completely when doing this. By varying the distance of the free hand from the instrument and the speed of movement it's possible to create a number of different sounds in this way, from cowboy campfire to spacy chorus effects.

WAH WAH

The "chamber" around the harp is opened and closed while playing, similar to a slow tremolo. Opening it creates a "Wah" effect. When your hands are closed, take care to get as good a seal as possible around the harp in order to maximize the effect when you open them. If you try doing this twice in succession, you get the well-known "wah wah" or "call your mama" sound often heard from Sonny Terry or Sonny Boy Williamson II. Naturally the timing of effects like this is very important in obtaining maximum impact. It can also help to silently form the syllables in your mouth at the same time. This effect works best on the lower draw notes.

Big Mama Thornton

Trills

Rapidly alternating between two adjacent blow or draw notes is often referred to as a "trill". It's best to start on the lower of the two. Move slowly up to the next note, and then back again a few times before trying to increase speed. You can produce this effect either by rapidly shaking your head, or by moving the hand holding the harp from side to side. If you only move your head or your hand, however, you'll find it's difficult to get the trill sounding smooth and regular. It's best to move both head and hand slightly, as they then traverse shorter distances, and the trill is therefore easier to control. A great additional effect can be attained by simultaneously bending the notes down, and up again. Try this on holes 3&4 draw or 4&5 draw.

Double Notes

Double notes are produced by enlarging the aperture of the lips so that they enclose two adjacent holes (e.g. 3&4 draw), which can then be played simultaneously. This sounds best when the interval between the two is a minor or a major third (either 3 or 4 semitones), as do trills. Often one note - usually the deeper of the two - is given more emphasis (i.e. more air). This effect is very popular among blues players as it gives a full, heavy sound, especially when combined with vibrato. As with trills, many double notes can also be bent, and both effects are often combined with Wah Wah.

Octaving, Splitting (Double Stops)

If you widen the aperture of your lips, so that they enclose four holes, and block the middle two with your tongue (see diagram), then only the outer two can sound.

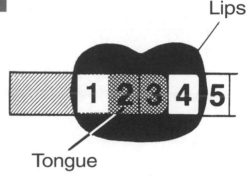

Lips

Tongue

In this way it's possible to play a number of useful intervals - e.g. octaves (1&4 blow, 1&4 draw, 2&5 blow, 3&6 blow) or sevenths (2&5 draw). These combinations in particular are often used in blues playing, either for extra punch (brass-type riffs) or to add musical tension. If the lips enclose three channels, and you block the middle one with your tongue (splitting), you can play other intervals such as fifths (2&4 draw, 1&3 blow), fourths (6&8 draw) or sixths (1&3 draw, 2&4 blow).

Glissando

Two sorts of glissandi (slides) are possible on the harp. One we have already discussed - sliding the pitch of certain notes down and up again by means of bending. The other type involves starting on one note, and gliding evenly over the intervening channels to the desired end note (all blow or all draw notes as a rule). The intervening notes sound rapidly one after another, in arpeggio (broken chords). An example would be to slide from 2 draw to 5 draw.

Rhythmic Effects

You can produce some great chord patterns by breathing rhythmically in and out through two or three channels simultaneously - try this, for example:

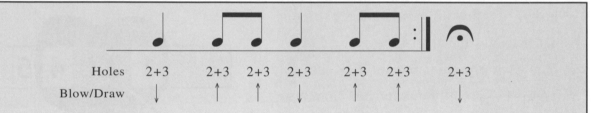

This is an excellent basis for the well-known train imitation pieces if you learn to do it fast enough. Here are a couple of variations on this theme to really get your train rolling:

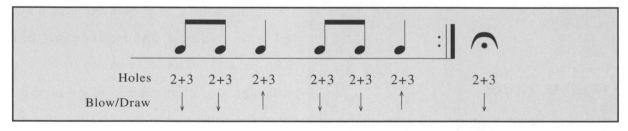

Or like this:

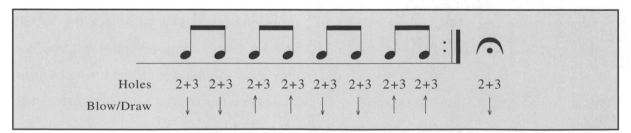

It's very important to end exercises like these on the draw chord in channels 1-3, and let the chord ring out for a while. That's what this sign means: .

If you combine these different rhythmic figures, and let your train speed up and slow down again, you already have a fairly varied "Train Blues" in your repertoire! The limits are set by your own fantasy - you can run through fields, over level crossings or even into tunnels. If you use your hands as well as your breathing to modulate the sound you can make it brighter and darker, louder and quieter again. The typical train whistle effect is produced by playing 3&4 draw or 4&5 draw as a double note. This will sound even more authentic if you form a Wah Wah with your hands, and bend the notes up at the same time. Let it roll!

With rhythmic exercises it's especially important to play in time - a good tip is to try to count the beats while playing, 12341234, in order to develop a feel for this.

CD-Track 21

Other interesting rhythmic effects can be created by forming silent syllables in the mouth whilst playing chords. The rhythm is accentuated more clearly like this than if produced by breathing alone.

CD-Track 22

"Two Rhythm Licks" / Dieter Kropp

Here is a figure which is really useful as rhythmic accompaniment over a shuffle beat, and can be used over a whole 12 bar verse:

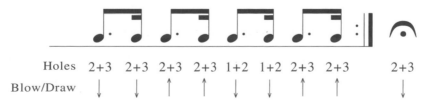

CD-Track 22

"Two Rhythm Licks" / Dieter Kropp

Here is an additional variation:

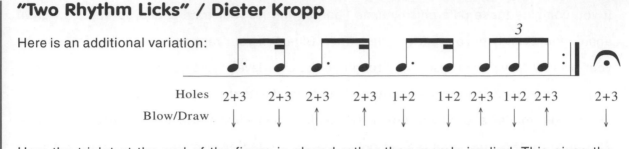

Holes	2+3	2+3	2+3	2+3	1+2	1+2	2+3	1+2	2+3	2+3
Blow/Draw	↓	↓	↑	↑	↓	↓	↑	↓	↑	↓

Here the triplet at the end of the figure is played rather than merely implied. This gives the whole thing more character. Try to get the triplet feel of the shuffle when you play these:

<u>da</u> da da <u>da</u> da da <u>da</u> da da <u>da</u> da da <u>da</u> da da <u>da</u> da da <u>da</u> da da <u>da</u> da da...

1   2   3   4   1   2   3   4

What this means is that while counting a normal 4/4 rhythm - 1-2-3-4-etc. - you should try to divide each beat into three triplets, to accentuate the shuffle feeling. It can help to form the silent syllables "da-da-da" while playing.

CD-Track 23

The following title demonstrates various rhythmic figures:

"Chugging" / Steve Baker

- Rhythmic number in G -

It's also possible to colour the sound by forming different vowel shapes in the mouth. This is one of the things which make the instrument so attractive - good players can often mimic the human voice on the harp, making it laugh, cry or scream by forming different syllables. Charlie Musselwhite once said that for him playing harp is just a way of using the instrument to talk or sing - simply as a means of expression. It's not necessary to vocalize the sounds, but to think them, and to form the mouth accordingly whilst playing a note on the harp. This technique can be used to vary the sound, to give it character - the harp can tell whole blues stories in just a few notes, and communicate the appropriate mood to the listener (and the player!).

It's worth experimenting a bit to see which syllables and vowels, which rhythmic patterns you like best. They can be used to great effect as accompaniment or when playing solo; everyone has their favourite tricks here, that work best for them, and the idea is that you find out what works best for you.

The Richter harmonica was originally designed to be played in the key of the blow chord - in C on a C harp, a.k.a. 1st position or straight harp. However, it's possible (and indeed usual) to play on one harp in various different keys or modes (harp players usually refer to these as "positions"). We have already gotten to know two of these modes - 1st position (see above) and 2nd position or cross harp (playing in G on a C harp). Basically it depends which of the notes available from the C major scale we take as our starting point; in 1st position we took C as our root note. In 2nd position we went up five notes (a fifth) and took G as our root note. If we continue this process, and go up another fifth, we come to D.

Charlie Musselwhite

3rd Position: D minor Dorian

If you take D (4 draw) as your root note, you get the following scale in the middle octave:

CD-Track 24

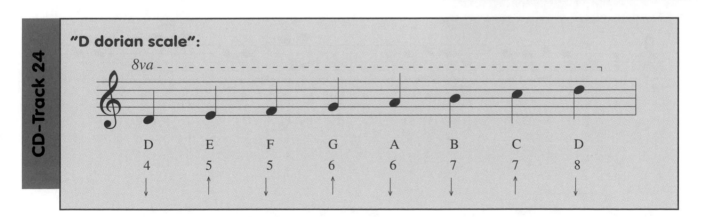

"D dorian scale":

D	E	F	G	A	B	C	D
4	5	5	6	6	7	7	8
↓	↑	↓	↑	↓	↓	↑	↓

This is called a dorian scale. It has a minor third (F) and a minor 7th (C), but the sixth note (B) is major, which gives the scale both minor and major characteristics. Like the G mixolydian scale mentioned earlier, it consists of the same notes as the C major scale, but starts and finishes on D.

Because 6 draw can be bent fairly easily to produce the "blue note" diminished fifth (Ab) in D, it's quite possible to play bluesy in 3rd position. The blues scale in D then looks like this:

Blues Scale in D:

CD-Track 24

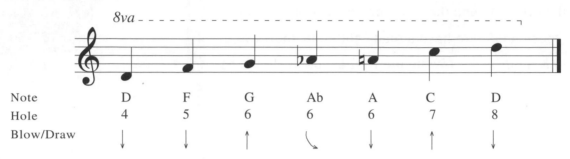

Note	D	F	G	Ab	A	C	D
Hole	4	5	6	6	6	7	8
Blow/Draw	↓	↓	↑	↘	↓	↑	↓

The 3rd position is great for many blues numbers in major keys, because with blues it's possible, or indeed normal, to play a minor instead of a major 3rd (here F instead of F#). It's also very good for rocky or melodic numbers in minor keys.

"Make Mine A Minor" / Steve Baker

- 12 bar blues in D, 3rd Position -

CD-Track 25

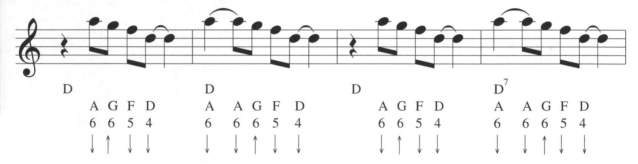

	D					D					D				D^7				
	A	G	F	D		A	A	G	F	D	A	G	F	D	A	A	G	F	D
	6	6	5	4		6	6	6	5	4	6	6	5	4	6	6	6	5	4
	↓	↑	↓	↓		↓	↓	↑	↓	↓	↓	↑	↓	↓	↓	↓	↑	↓	↓

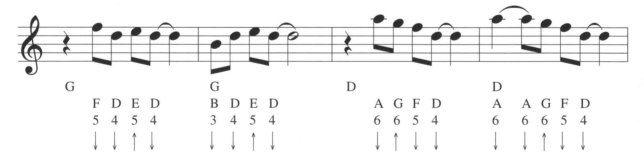

G					G					D					D				
F	D	E	D		B	D	E	D		A	G	F	D		A	A	G	F	D
5	4	5	4		3	4	5	4		6	6	5	4		6	6	6	5	4
↓	↓	↑	↓		↓	↓	↑	↓		↓	↑	↓	↓		↓	↓	↑	↓	↓

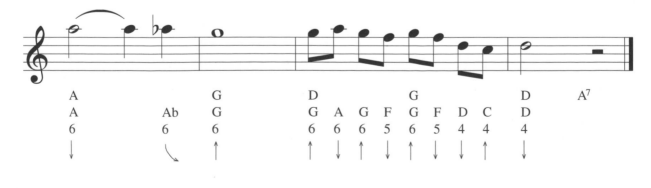

A		G		D		G					D			A^7
A		Ab		G		G	A	G	F	G	F	D	C	D
6		6		6		6	6	6	5	6	5	4	4	4
↓		↘		↑		↑	↓	↑	↓	↑	↓	↓	↑	↓

4th Position: A minor Aeolian ("natural minor")

To find 4th position we go up another fifth, from D to A (6 draw or 3 draw bent a whole tone), and take that as our root note. If the notes of the C major scale are played through, starting and finishing on A, then the resulting scale is the classic minor scale in A, which has no major character at all, and is often referred to as "natural minor". A minor is the parallel minor scale to C major.

A minor scale over 2 octaves:

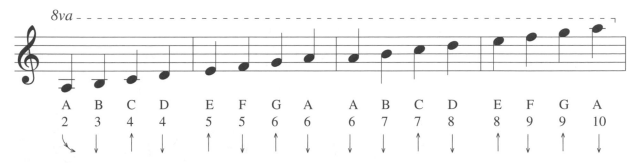

Generally speaking this position is best suited for melody playing in minor keys.

5th Position: E minor phrygian

E minor scale over 2 octaves:

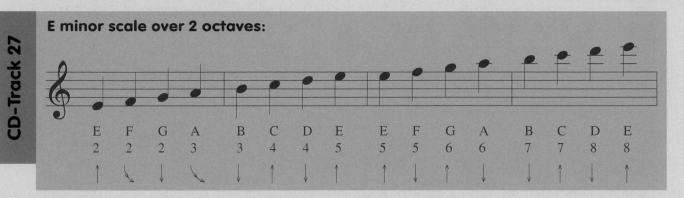

If the notes of the C major scale are played through taking E as the root note (a fifth up from A), we get what is called a phrygian scale in the middle octave - a minor scale with a diminished 2nd (F instead of F#), which has a very "Spanish" sound.

By leaving out the diminished 2nd (F) and 6th (C), we get a minor pentatonic scale with the same notes as the G major pentatonic, but with E as the root note. Clearly the 5th position is closely related to the 2nd - E minor is the parallel minor scale to G major.

This position is great for bluesy or rocky numbers in minor keys, but also for melodic pieces.

Positions Table for diatonic harps in all keys

Key of harp	Key in which you play				
	1st Position	2nd Position	3rd Position	4th Position	5th Position
	=	=	=	=	=
	"Straight"/ Major Ionian	"Crossed"/blues Mixolydian	"Double Crossed" Dorian	"Natural Minor" Aeolian	"Minor" Phrygian
G	G	D	A^m	E^m	B^m
A^b	A^b	E^b	B^{bm}	F^m	C^m
A	A	E	B^m	F$^{\#m}$	C$^{\#m}$
B^b	B^b	F	C^m	G^m	D^m
B	B	F$^\#$	C$^{\#m}$	A^{bm}/G$^{\#m}$	E^{bm}/D$^{\#m}$
C	C	G	D^m	A^m	E^m
D^b	D^b	A^b	E^{bm}	B^{bm}	F^m
D	D	A	E^m	B^m	F$^{\#m}$
E^b	E^b	B^b	F^m	C^m	G^m
E	E	B	F$^{\#m}$	C$^{\#m}$	A^{bm}/G$^{\#m}$
F	F	C	G^m	D^m	A^m
F$^\#$	F$^\#$	C$^\#$	A^{bm}/G$^{\#m}$	E^{bm}/D$^{\#m}$	B^{bm}/A$^{\#m}$

The harp was first amplified in the early fifties with the advent of urban (Chicago) blues. The technique of amplifying the harp through a hand-held microphone plugged into a guitar amp (to give it a chance of competing against drums, bass and electric guitar in the volume stakes) has survived to this day, and is also often used in rock music. If you play (or want to play) with a band, or just like the sound, it can be well worth trying.

An interesting set-up! '59 Fender Bassman, '63 Fender Reverb, Astatic JT 30, Hohner Marine Band.

The size of the amplifier depends on your requirements (and your bank balance!): how loud you want (or need) to play, what degree of distortion you want, and whether you prefer a valve (tube) or transistor sound. The great majority of experienced harp players prefer tube amps such as the Fender Super Reverb, Fender Bassman or Fender Champ. Old Gibson amps can also be very good. Today a number of manufacturers such as Fender, Peavey and Ampeg have brought out "reissues" of tube amps from the late fifties and early sixties, some of which are excellent for electric harp. The best thing to do is go along to a reputable music store and try a few out, using the same microphone you intend to use later. Don't turn the input volume, distortion or tone controls up too high, or you're likely to experience problems with feedback. It can be good to use an amp with a built-in reverb unit, as this makes for a fuller, rounder sound.

The choice of microphone also depends on a number of factors - it's very important that you can hold it comfortably with the harp, and that it's not too heavy when playing for long periods of time. The "bicycle lamp"-type mikes such as the Astatic JT30, Hohner Blues Blaster or Shure Green Bullet sit easily in the hand, and are

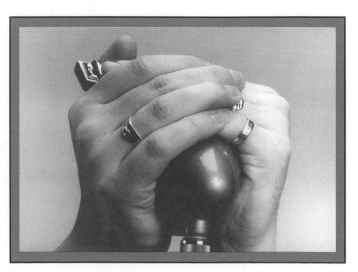

good for a distorted sound. They distort by different amounts, though, and have rather different frequency characteristics, so it's advisable to test them to see which one you prefer.

A normal vocal mike such as the Shure SM58 is better if you want a clean sound. This type of mike is also best if you don't want any distortion at all, but simply want to make your acoustic sound loud enough (over a small PA, for example) to suit the size and ambient noise level of the room you're playing in. In this case play in front of the mike, about 2-4 inches away, and don't hold it in your hands. This enables you to use the hand effects discussed in the previous chapter.

Although an amplifier can be very useful when playing in a band, it's absolutely vital to remember that you have to create the sound yourself. Don't just expect the amp to do all the work, because it won't! You should always practice at getting a good acoustic tone, and then use the amp to find an electric sound that suits you.

9 Influential Players

When you start learning to play harp, it's essential to listen as much as possible to how the master players sound, and how they use the instrument. The only way to become really familiar with the music, and the role the harp plays in it, is to hear it constantly over a long period of time. For this reason, we've put together a small and necessarily incomplete discography of some of the most influential players, which ought at least to give you a starting point.

Listening to other players, and other techniques and styles, has always been indispensable for blues harpists; this is more the case than with other instruments, since harmonica literature and sheet music is fairly rare and sometimes of dubious quality. Most of the great players started by picking up tips from other musicians, or spending nights in clubs and bars listening to their idols, and trying to imitate them. Learning by listening and learning by doing are the only two ways to get anywhere on the harp! Don't just try to copy other players note for note, though. You should give yourself the possibility of developing your own style once you've mastered the basics, to find your own means of expression with the help of what you've learned and heard. The history of the harp's not over yet!

Influential players and their recordings. This list is by no means complete and is just meant to give an overall view.

Traditional Blues

Sonny Boy Williamson I. John Lee "Sonny Boy" Williamson was one of the first great stars of the blues harmonica, and his influence on almost all those who came after him was enormous. In the course of his 10 year recording career from 1937 until shortly before his death in 1948, he recorded over 120 songs, many of which have become classics of the genre. 24 of them can be heard on the compilation "Sugar Mama", CD Indigo IGO 2014. If you need more, try "The Complete Recorded Works in Chronological Order", Vols. 1-5, Document Records DOCD 5055 - 5059.

Noah Lewis was one of the greatest pioneers of country blues harmonica. He was the first to really establish it as lead instrument in a band situation. His melodic style uses both 1st and 2nd positions. His few solo recordings, and those with the Noah Lewis Jugband, are great, but his finest work can be heard on his earlier recordings with Gus Cannon. The CD "Gus Cannon & His Jug Stompers (1928 - 30)", JSP 610, contains high quality versions of the classic tracks, and has been re-released at the time of writing.

Sonny Terry and guitarist/singer Brownie McGhee were undoubtedly the best known country blues duo ever. They played together for over 40 years, and their better recordings define the genre. Sonny is perhaps the most important of all the traditional acoustic players, and his remarkable "whooping", incorporated seamlessly into his melodic lines and sung through the harp, is truly unique. EMI have recently re-released the recordings for Capitol Records from 1947 - 50, in excellent quality and with extensive liner notes: "Whoopin' The Blues - The Capitol Recordings" EMI 8 29372 2.

Great stuff! Also good is "Midnight Special", ACE CH 951.

Sonny Boy Williamson II. Rice Miller, or "Sonny Boy Williamson II", as he is better known, embodies the blues myth as do few others. He was a drifter for much of his life, and stole the name of his more famous namesake in the early 1940s in order to capitalize on John Lee's reputation (something which caused much bad feeling amongst other musicians). He began playing harp aged five, picking up tips at parties, but was first recorded in the early fifties in Jackson, Mississippi by the Trumpet label, when about 50 years old. He must be one of the most expressive harmonica players who ever lived. His most famous recordings were made later in Chicago for Chess/Checker. The most interesting 44 titles from 1955 - 64 are on "The Essential Sonny Boy Williamson II", MCA/Chess CHD2 9343.

Little Walter is arguably the most important post-war harp player, some would say the best ever! Born Marion Walter Jacobs in 1930 in Marksville, Louisiana, circumstances forced him to start using his remarkable talent on the harmonica to earn his own living at an early age. As a twelve year old he was already playing for tips on the streets of New Orleans, and he arrived in Chicago at the age of 17 in the late forties. In the course of the next few years, the combination of Walter's already phenomenal instrumental abilities, and the encouragement he received from established figures on the Chicago scene such as Muddy Waters and Jimmy Rogers, led him to develop what was to become a whole new tradition for blues harmonica.

Although his early recordings clearly show the influence of John Lee Williamson, it was his discovery of the amazing sounds which could be created by amplifying the harp through a cheap microphone and a guitar amplifier which really helped him create his own inimitable style. Walter extended the tradition enormously: he was the first great blues harmonica innovator - a thoroughly modern player in the 1950's! Walter played harp in Muddy Waters' band during the early 50's, until the sudden commercial success of his first solo recording "Juke", an instrumental which Muddy's band used as a theme tune, in 1952. He rapidly left Muddy and formed his own group, "Little Walter & The Aces", which became almost a blueprint for the classic Chicago blues band. The majority of Little Walter's recordings (he was also a gifted vocalist) are quite simply brilliant, and his influence on subsequent generations of players cannot be overstated. Tragically, he

died at the early age of 38 from injuries sustained in a fight, but his legacy lives on today in the playing of thousands of blues musicians to whom he is still one of the greatest sources of inspiration. The lovingly presented compilation "The Essential Little Walter" (MCA/Chess CHD2 9342) contains all his best work. A must!

Junior Wells took over the harp chair in Muddy Waters' band after the departure of Little Walter. The Aces used to be Junior's backing band - he got the job with Muddy, and Walter got the Aces! Apart from his early solo recordings, many of his finest moments seem to have been with guitarist Buddy Guy, with whom he recorded the excellent "Hoodoo Man Blues" in 1965 (Delmark CD DD 612). He was still recording shortly before his death in early 1998.

Walter Horton, also known as "Big Walter" or "Shakey Horton", was a great musician who sadly never received the recognition he deserved during his lifetime. His unique and powerful tone on the harp made him one of the most expressive performers on the instrument. Undoubtedly much of his best work was as an accompanist - the classic example has to be his breathtaking solo on the original version of "Walking By Myself" by Jimmy Rogers. However, many of his recordings under his own name are also milestones in blues history. His instrumental "Easy", recorded in 1953 in Sam Phillips' Sun Studios, is a classic of its kind. The album "Blues Harp Maestro" (ACE CDCH 252)

Sonny Terry

contains great material recorded in Memphis during early 1951, and "Fine Cuts" (Blind Pig BP 70678) is a varied and interesting selection from later in Horton's career which is also highly recommended. Masterpieces from the "Master of Tone"!

Paul Butterfield. Together with Charlie Musselwhite, Paul Butterfield was one of the groundbreaking white blues harpists who brought the real Chicago blues to a young white audience in the mid sixties. His first album "The Paul Butterfield Blues Band" (Elektra CD 18P2 2696) is one of the finest blues records of that period. Later he experimented with jazz-rock and soul influences - "East - West" (Elektra 7315 2) is a good example. Amongst his finest recordings are two albums from the early 70's, under the name of "Paul Butterfield's Better Days": "Better Days" (NEX 127) and "It All Comes Back" (NEX 128). Sadly the better days didn't last too long, and Butterfield died in May 1987. He remains one of the most influential players of his generation.

Charlie Musselwhite undoubtedly occupies a special position among the top white American harp players - a kind of elder statesman of the blues. Born in Kosciusko/Mississippi in 1944, he grew up with the blues as a part of everyday life. As a boy in Memphis he encountered country blues legends Furry Lewis and Will Shade, the harp player with the Memphis Jug Band, which made a lasting impression on him. Later Charlie took the typical Southern migrant's road in search of work, and headed north for Chicago, where he was befriended by Robert Jr. Lockwood, Johnny Young and Homesick James. He was accepted from an early stage by the black Chicago blues musicians whose southern roots he shared, and with whom he soon began playing. His expressive and technically polished harmonica style grew out of this background. "The Harmonica According To Charlie Musselwhite" (Blind Pig BPCD 5016) was recorded in England in 1978, and demonstrates a number of styles and positions on the harp. "In My Time" (Alligator ALCD 4818), released to coincide with his 50th birthday, is probably his finest work to date. Here he has succeeded not only in capturing some great music on record, but also in creating an atmosphere of rare intensity and power. A true masterpiece from one of the greats!

Kim Wilson is considered by many to be the finest exponent of traditional blues harmonica (and one of the finest white vocalists) recording and performing today. His work with The Fabulous Thunderbirds from Austin, Texas was enormously influential during the late 70's and early 80's, and spawned a host of imitators. In the 90's he has at the time of writing produced three excellent solo albums and a very fine CD with legendary Chicago guitarist Jimmy Rogers, all of which showcase his benchmark harp playing. He is one of the

Sonny Boy Williamson II

very few musicians on any instrument who are masters of the blues tradition without ever sounding like they're simply recycling it, and he plays with an effortless authority which gives every note a totally personal touch. The seminal early albums by the Fabulous Thunderbirds have recently been re-released: "Girls Go Wild/What's The Word" (Chrysalis, CD BGOCD 192), and his three solo albums "Tiger Man" (Antone's, CD ANT 0023), "That's Life" (Antone's, CD ANT 0034) and "My Blues" (Blue Collar Music, BCM 7107)show him at the height of his powers. In 1997 Kim founded his own record company, Blues Collar Music, and his most recent Solo CD "My Blues" is the first release on this new blues label. Outstanding production, crystal clear sound. The music pays loving tribute to a range of '50s, blues styles with a level of authenticity which makes it one of the finest traditional blues albums of the 90's.

Here are some interesting compilation albums featuring a wide variety of blues harp players and styles which provide a good introduction to the music:

Rhino Blues Masters Vol. 4:
Harmonica Classics (CD 71124 2)

A solid introduction to the history of post-war blues harp. From Little Walter's "Juke" to Walter Horton's "Easy" to Charlie Musselwhite or the Fabulous Thunderbirds, here you get a cross section of trendsetting harp titles from some of the most important players dating from the early 50's to the early 80's, as well as an informative booklet.

Got Harp If You Want It
(CrossCut CCD 11030)

The best of the West Coast blues harp players. Good 80's compilation album featuring many of today's top players such as Rick Estrin, Mark Ford or William Clarke as well as the hitherto unknown (to us at least - *the authors*) Paul Durkett, whose breathtaking version of the Jerry McCain classic "Steady" is one of the highlights of this excellent album.

Blues Harp Boogie
(Red Lightnin' / Music Collection International CD MC 124)

Various artists, black and white, on recordings from the 50's to the 80's including Charlie Musselwhite, Paul De Lay, Jimmy Reed and many others. Good stuff.

Over the last 20 years, a considerable number of "modern" harmonica players have emerged who have gone beyond the traditional blues framework and are taking the instrument into new territory. Unfortunately, many of their recordings are even harder to find than those of the blues players, which has to a certain extent dictated the choice of the following small selection.

Norton Buffalo is a virtuoso country-oriented modern harp stylist from the West Coast who has little in common with the California blues players. He is probably best known to a wider audience for his work with Steve Miller. In the late 70's he released two solo albums, "Lovin' in the Valley of the Moon" (1977) and "Desert Horizon" (1978), which have recently been re-released on one double CD (Edsel 431). These albums are more in the singer/songwriter tradition, and mix country/ folk/blues/rock elements in a very 70s Californian way. Recently he has recorded with slide guitarist (and John Lee Hooker producer) Roy Rogers, with whom he also performs live. These albums are still available, and provide a good introduction to his style. Roy Rogers & Norton Buffalo: "Travellin' Tracks" (Blind Pig CD BP 5003), "R&B" (Blind Pig CD BP 74491).

Magic Dick, harp player with the legendary J. Geils Band, was the first to successfully integrate the harp into a rock 'n' roll context and really make it part of the band sound. He can be heard on all of their albums from 1970 until the mid 80's. Now he has returned to playing traditional Chicago blues with his band "Bluestime" (featuring J. Geils on guitar), which is where he began, but his work with the J. Geils Band makes him essential listening for anyone interested in rock harmonica. Atlantic has recently released a 2 CD compilation set containing all their best material plus a 50 page booklet: "The J. Geils Band Anthology" (Atlantic CD 71164 2).

Howard Levy is considered by many to be the most technically accomplished diatonic harmonica player on the planet. He is certainly the best-known pioneer of overblowing, the technique necessary to get all the missing chromatic notes out of the harp. This man can play any tune (we're talking bebop here!) in any key you care to name on any key harp you like, a fairly remarkable achievement. He has recorded with numerous artists in many styles, ranging from the country rock of Dolly Parton and Kenny Loggins to Rabih Abu Kahlil's ethno-jazz, and was recently signed by the highly reputable American jazz label Blue Note. His work with Bela Fleck and the Flecktones is interesting, and don't miss his Blue Note album when it comes out! "Bela Fleck and the Flecktones" (Warner Bros. CD 9 26124-2), Kenny Loggins "Outside from the Redwoods/live" (Columbia 474347-2).

Charlie McCoy was the no.1 studio harp in Nashville for almost two decades, where he accompanied virtually everybody who ever recorded there (i.e. virtually everybody in country music!), and must be the most widely known country harp player. His style is clean and often very fast, as his well known version of the fiddle tune "Orange Blossom Special" testifies. His solo albums may be too syrupy for mainstream rock and blues fans, but his playing on the recordings of other artists is excellent. "Greatest Hits" (MC 7622) and "Nashville Platinum" (FC 40440) showcase his style.

Lee Oskar started his career with Eric Burdon and the seminal funk outfit War, with whom he recorded numerous albums as well as releasing solo projects. An excellent player with an instantly recognisable sound, he has been instrumental in integrating the diatonic harp into a wide variety of musical styles, and is also a pioneer of the use of electronic effects and alternative tunings. His early solo albums "Lee Oskar" (Rhino 71719), "Before The Rain" (Rhino 71721) and "My Road Our Road" (Rhino 71720) have been re-released on CD, and Rhino Records has recently also put out several of the War albums on CD.

For a detailed discography, as well as much in-depth information for more advanced players which would lie outside the scope of this book, see "The Harp Handbook" by Steve Baker (English edition), distributed by Music Sales and Hohner. Hohner Publishing also stocks a number of the more important harmonica recordings - a list can be obtained by writing to Matth. Hohner AG - Verlag, Postfach 1258, 78636 Trossingen, Germany.

The most useful sources for the above-mentioned recordings will be the mail order catalogues from CrossCut Records, Postfach 106524, 28065 Bremen, Germany, tel. (49) 421 168020, fax (49) 421 168021, and Red Lick Records, Porthmadog LL49 9DJ, Gwynedd, GB-Wales.

Another highly interesting book, written with much love and attention to detail, is "Harmonicas, Harps and Heavy Breathers" by Kim Field (A Fireside Book, published by Simon & Schuster, New York, ISBN 0-671-79633-X). It chronicles the musical history of the instrument in the USA and features a wealth of interviews and portraits of the top players in the most varied styles including Little Walter, Toots Thielemans, Kim Wilson, Larry Adler and many others. Essential reading!

In recent years a number of harmonica fanzines have emerged which are primarily directed at the blues harmonica player. The journalistic standard has improved immeasurably, and the publications listed below are thoroughly recommended. We have also included some addresses of companies specialising in mail order harmonicas and accessories:

American Harmonica Newsmagazine (AHN), Al Eichler (editor),104 Highland Avenue,
Battle Creek, MI 49015-3272, USA
AHN is the only monthly harmonica periodical in the world, and is highly recommended.

Harmonica Information Publication (HIP), Winslow T. Yerxa, 203 14th Avenue,
San Francisco, CA 94118, USA
HIP hasn't appeared regularly over the last couple of years but is extremely interesting when it does.

Harmonica World, Colin Mort (editor), Rivendell, Shirrel Heath,
Southampton SO32 2JN, GB

Harmonica World is the official publication of the National Harmonica League.

There is a well-subscribed Harp List in the Internet which is used by numerous harmonica devotees worldwide for the exchange of information, and can be reached by sending an E-mail to: <majordomo@garply.com> using the subject <subscribe harp-l> or <subscribe harp-l-digest>. The archive can be reached on the Internet under <http://www.garply.com/harp-l/archives>

HarpCity, P.O. Box 884, Babylon NY 11702-0884, USA,
Tel. ++1-516-321-7422, Fax 516-587-9179
http://www.harp-city.com

Kevins Harps sells everything connected with the harmonica worldwide by mail order and accepts all major credit cards. Great selection, keen prices.

J&R Farrell Company, P.O. Box 133, Harrisburg OH 43126-0133, USA
Tel. ++1-800-438-3543, Fax 614-877-1714

Farrell is another reliable harmonica mail order company.

Carey Bell

11 | Playing With Other Musicians

Whether you play in a duo with a guitarist, or in a big band, your first duty as a musician is always to listen to the others, in order to fit your playing to theirs. It really isn't usually necessary to play right through a song from beginning to end, or to try to play the maximum number of notes in the shortest possible time. Learning to listen will help you to develop sensitivity for what the other musicians are doing, so that you can react appropriately. The most important thing about a piece of music is that everything has to sound good together! Try to play with feeling, and keep the complete song in mind rather than just your role in it - you'll get your chance for a solo too! A good motto to remember is everything in its place and at the right time.

12 | Care and Maintenance

You can prolong the life of your harps considerably if you take proper care of them. The following tips should help you here:

Warm the harp in your hands, or by breathing lightly into it, before you play it, so that the reeds are not subjected to the stress of playing when cold.

New harps should be played in gradually - play softly, and don't do any heavy bending at first. The instrument needs time to become broken in to the way you play.

It's a good idea to play with your head in an upright position and a clean, fairly dry mouth so that saliva doesn't run into the harp and clog the reeds. Tap it out from time to time while playing to prevent this. Playing immediately after eating can easily cause reeds to stick - small particles of food and other gunk can lodge between reed and reed plate. If this happens, try knocking the harp out into the palm of your hand, or gently lift the reed in question (be careful or you'll break it - Hohner accepts no liability for such damage) with a piece of wire or thin blade so that the offending object can be extracted.

Always knock the harp out in the palm of your hand after playing, to prevent saliva from collecting in it and causing rust. Let it dry, and then put it back in the case.

Take it out again soon though!!

Steve Baker & Dieter Kropp

Blues Harping, Volume 2
Steve Baker / Dieter Kropp / Lars Luis Linek

HOHNER Verlag Trossingen, Cat.-No. 00.091.126

This book/MC package offers a unique learning opportunity for the more advanced harmonica player. Six instrumental titles (two by each of the authors) ranging in style from Blues and Rhythm & Blues to Swing and Bossa Nova are to be heard on the MC, first with harp plus backing, and then as playbacks for you to play along with. Top quality professional accompaniment from Rainer Baumann and Dick Bird (guitars), Christoph Buhse (drums) and Thomas Jahnke (bass) makes practicing a pleasure! Each title consists of a theme (head) which is usually played twice, followed by a four chorus improvisation, after which the theme is repeated at the end. In the book the complete themes are transcribed in musical notation and harmonica tablature plus chords, with an accompanying text written by the composer for each title, containing tips and exercises to make the pieces easier to learn. All songs are played on a C harp.

The Harp Handbook - Steve Baker

Edition Louis/Music Sales, available from HOHNER Verlag Trossingen, Cat.-No. 30.108.972
The encyclopedia of the diatonic harmonica! Virtually every important aspect of the instrument from the viewpoint of the diatonic blues player is dealt with at length in this remarkable book which has been praised as the "harmonica player's bible". Early history, construction, bending and overblowing, the different positions, playing techniques, styles, amplification, musical history and development, special tunings and much more. There is also an extensive discography plus a detailed chapter on tuning and maintenance, and 16 pages of exercises including practice material for all the first five positions and several special tunings. The cult book!

Harmonicas - Types, Techniques, Tonalities
Steve Baker / Hermann Demmler

HOHNER Verlag Trossingen, Cat.-No. 00.170.181

This book fills a long overdue gap in harmonica literature, and within a very short space of time has become the standard work on the subject. After a short history of the instrument the authors explain the underlying musical principles shared by all the various types of harmonica, using their concept of the "central octave" as a common denominator. Thereafter separate chapters deal with the technical and musical characteristics and peculiarities of chromatic harmonicas, Richter models (blues harps), Wiener octave models, tremolo harmonicas, and finally group and orchestra instruments. An additional chapter answering "questions frequently asked about the harmonica" offers practical help in many matters of maintenance and will save the reader much time and trouble.

Selected Discography

"Have Mercy" - HAVE MERCY

With up to three harmonicas at once an unusual treat for all harp fans. Produced by Steve Baker, who is joined by his old friends and colleagues Henry Heggen and Rory McLeod on harmonica and vocals, plus Brian Barnett and Dick Bird on guitars and mandolin and vocals for this award winning all-acoustic CD on CrossCut Records. Have Mercy - the first non-American act ever to be signed by Germany's premier blues label - play what they call "Rocking Harmonica Blues" with enormous energy and conviction. Although their music is firmly rooted in the Jugband tradition, it also draws on influences from other forms of black American music from the 20's to the 50's. This is not just a band, it's more a way of life and a whole basic approach to playing music, which can probably best be described as "you always give absolutely everything you've got".

Cat-No.: 08.100.145

"Slow Roll" - STEVE BAKER & CHRIS JONES

Steve Baker produced this highly praised album with Chris Jones, a remarkable guitarist and singer who originally hails from Reno, Nevada. "Slow Roll" (Acoustic Music Records) shines through the extremely personal choice of songs, and the intensity and virtuosity of their interpretation. Powerful and well thought out, it features Steve playing some of the most interesting harmonica work of his 20 year recording career. Chris and Steve are masters of their instruments on a very high level, but the driving force behind their music is an intensity which goes far beyond technical expertise. Together they generate a compelling energy which is much more than just the sum of its parts, and in doing so they stretch the boundaries of their music into new realms. Stylistically this album is extremely varied, but Jones and Baker succeed in giving every number an unmistakable quality of their own which ensures continuity. It ranges from country blues to haunting ballads, and from minimalist funk to crunching rockers. Seven of the titles are self-penned, and the remainder are culled from sources as diverse as Leadbelly, Z.Z. Top, Bonnie Raitt or J.J. Cale. They all bear an indelible stamp of authority. **Cat-No.: 08.100.011**

MEINERT & KROPP - "innocence is gone"

On "innocence is gone", Dieter Kropp and Mickey Meinert once again demonstrate their strong personal and musical affinity, combining respect for the great black and white masters of the blues with individual creativity to express their own feelings through the medium of the blues. This is a peaceful and relaxed album of blues and songs for listening rather than partying, lyrics alternate between English and German. Good old traditions coupled with creative new ideas make "innocence is gone" a truly unusual blues album an inspirational blues adventure.

Cat-No.: 08.100.066

THE FABULOUS BARBECUE BOYS
featuring Dieter Kropp - "...doin' the blues"

"... doin' the blues" is the recording debut of this Westphalian combo fronted by harp player and singer Dieter Kropp - a six track mini-CD, offering original material as well as covers of songs by Walter Horton and Sonny Boy Williamson II (Rice Miller). Dieter, the "master of the fat-toned harp", demonstrates that it is indeed possible for European bands to produce convincing versions of 50s blues classics. This recording combines feeling and love of the music to produce an album of exceptional authenticity.

Cat-No.: 08.100.082